A BIRTH MOM'S

JOURNEY THROUGH

ADOPTION

Michelle Lee Graham

Editor: Alexa Tanen

Illustrator: Yelyzaveta Serdyuk

Format: Rocio Monroy

Photographer: Stephanie Adkisson

To my first grandson, Thomas Jeffrey.

May you always know our story.

The clock read 8:00 pm; bedtime for Daniel, Jacob, and Rachel. Time to begin the nightly routine of tuck-ins, stories, and prayers.

Rachel snuggled into her warm blankets, her beautiful blue eyes peeking over the top, "Mommy, will you tell me, again, about my sister, Sarah?"

They loved to hear about their older sister and our adoption story.

"Once upon a time, before any of you were born, Mommy had another baby in her tummy. This baby, Sarah, was very special. She was my first.

"I loved her so much! I wanted Sarah to have all the things a little girl wants and needs to grow."

"I didn't have those things to give her because I was still a young girl, myself."

"I searched far and wide for a mom and dad who could give Sarah all she needed.
Finally, I found the perfect family for my little girl. They would love her as their very own.
This was my biggest job as her birth mom and, with God's help, we all became family!"

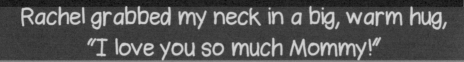

Rachel grabbed my neck in a big, warm hug,
"I love you so much Mommy!"

As the years went by, we anxiously awaited the pictures and letters from Sarah's family. We all loved to see them and read about Sarah's life.

On the holidays, we celebrated Sarah in special ways.
I would decorate an Easter egg with her name on it.
I hung her First Christmas ornament, every year,
on the tree. She was remembered in everything we did.

As the years went by,
I had two more children, Lauren and Mason.
Now, with a full house of five children,
the traditions of celebrating Sarah always continued.

The clock read 8:00 pm; bedtime for Lauren and Mason. Time to begin our nightly routine of tuck-ins, stories, and prayers.

MOONLIGHT

14

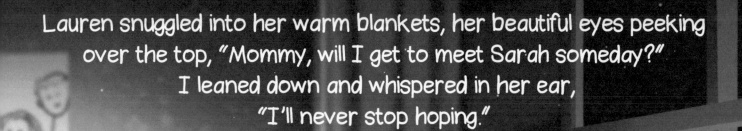

Lauren snuggled into her warm blankets, her beautiful eyes peeking over the top, "Mommy, will I get to meet Sarah someday?"
I leaned down and whispered in her ear,
"I'll never stop hoping."

Lauren grabbed my neck in a big, warm hug,
"I think Sarah would want to meet you!"

15

More years went by and, one day, instead of a letter from
Sarah's mom and dad, we received one from Sarah,
who was now all grown up. She wanted to meet us.

16

The day Sarah was to arrive,
everyone was excited.
She was family and had been
loved her whole life.

I was the most excited of all.

17

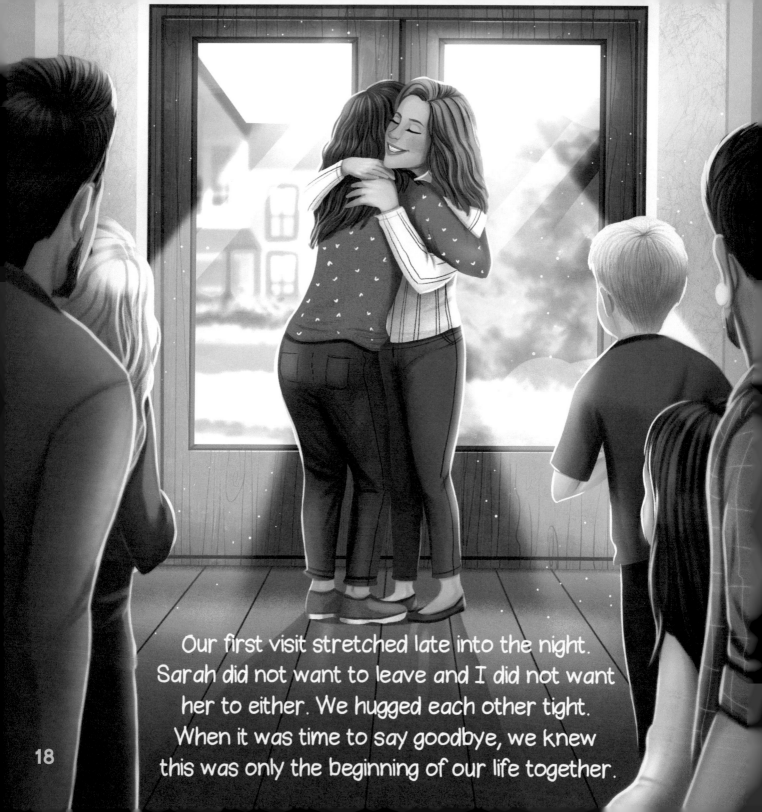

Our first visit stretched late into the night.
Sarah did not want to leave and I did not want
her to either. We hugged each other tight.
When it was time to say goodbye, we knew
this was only the beginning of our life together.

18

In the years that followed, Sarah and I continued to build
our special relationship.

We went on trips, celebrated holidays,
and talked every day.

One day, Sarah said the words that gave my heart such joy.

"I always knew you loved me!"

I will forever be thankful for Sarah's mom and dad,
and their reminders to Sarah of just how
much her birth mom loved her.

ABOUT THE AUTHOR

"I am proud to be a Birth Mom and share my personal story with you"

Michelle Lee
Graham

http://michelleleegraham.com/

A Child's Journey Through Adoption shows the daughter's perspective and the nurturing love that her adopted parents gave her. It showcases all of the beautiful reminders that she was always valued and loved from the very beginning of her life, both by them and her birth mom. Be prepared to experience a lovely story that spans a lifetime, offering a future of hope, love, and adoption like you always thought it could be.

OTHER TITLES BY MICHELLE :

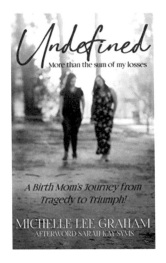

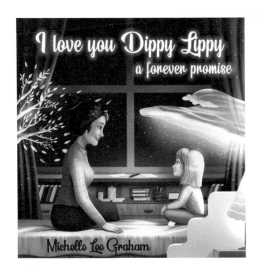

All books are available in Spanish

Available on

Scan the code to get your own copy

Made in the USA
Columbia, SC
26 February 2024